The Smoothie Recipe Book for Weight Loss

The Smoothie Recipe Book for Weight Loss

ADVICE & 72 EASY SMOOTHIES TO LOSE WEIGHT

MENDOCINO PRESS

Contents

Introduction

Taking off those extra pounds doesn't have to be uncomfortable or feel like a sacrifice. Drinking healthy smoothies not only is a delicious and satisfying approach to losing weight, but also provides you with a nutritious alternative to skipping meals or—worse yet—subjecting yourself to foods you just don't care for.

This book will teach you everything you need to know about making smoothies and using them to reach your weight-loss goals. You'll learn strategies for losing weight that are effective and easy.

It's imperative to understand the dos and don'ts of making smoothies that are specifically geared toward losing weight and keeping it off. Chapter 1 offers invaluable information about what and what not to include in your smoothies, as well as ten tips for making the best smoothies possible.

Chapter 2 addresses the nuts and bolts of how the nutrients in a healthy smoothie (along with exercise) will lead you down the path to success. Motivational tips are an added bonus.

Healthy weight loss and detoxifying the body go hand in hand. For an additional jump start to your weight-loss program, Chapter 3 contains a three-day menu plan composed entirely of cleansing smoothies for maximum results. This approach may be just the push you've been looking for.

Nutrient-dense, low-calorie dinners are a great accompaniment to a smoothie weight-loss program. Chapter 4 gives ten dinner ideas and highlights twenty smoothies you can enjoy for both breakfast and lunch.

Weight loss through incorporating healthful smoothies into your diet is just the first step into a new lifestyle. The health benefits and vitality you will experience when you begin eating fruits and vegetables will last a lifetime. The smoothies included here are linked to:

- The power of green
- Antioxidant-rich foods
- Lower-fat choices
- Higher-energy drinks
- Digestive health

These seventy-two recipes are easy to make and contain ingredients that are easy to find in your local grocery or health-food store.

HOW TO USE THIS BOOK

The Smoothie Recipe Book for Weight Loss can be used in a number of ways. If you enjoy smoothies but don't wish to lose weight, just use these recipes whenever you want. It's that simple!

If you *do* need to lose some weight, the smoothies in this book can be used in several ways:

1. As meal replacements
2. As a detox program (see Chapter 3)
3. As replacements for two meals a day for ten days (see Chapter 4)

An added benefit of this program is that you don't need to count calories. Each smoothie provides approximately one 16- to 24-ounce serving (depending upon how much liquid you add), has between 200 and 500 calories, and contains only a few grams of fat.

These recipes can be used as is or adapted by substituting your favorite fruits and vegetables. Here are a few caloric guidelines that can help when you're planning meals or changing ingredients:

- Unsweetened fruits contain very few calories (and virtually no fat).
  - Berries generally contain 25 to 45 calories per ½-cup serving.
  - The majority of other fruits have a calorie content closer to the high end of this range.
  - Bananas range from 72 to 135 calories, so always choose a smaller banana.
- Vegetables are extremely low in calories and also virtually fat-free.
- When adding liquids to your smoothies, water can always be substituted for milk. This results in fewer calories but less nutritional value.

CHAPTER 1

Smoothie Basics

It's essential to understand what a smoothie *is* before making one. Smoothies are usually thick, sometimes creamy concoctions puréed in a blender that consist of fresh and/or frozen fruit with some type of milk added.

This description is somewhat accurate, but a little outdated. Smoothies have changed quite a bit over the years, and these days most offer significantly more nutrition per glass. Smoothies now include a wide variety of fruits, some vegetables (primarily greens), healthy fats, and any number of different types of milks (or water).

Smoothies aren't just for breakfast anymore, either. By including your favorite ingredients, smoothies can be reminiscent of a favorite dessert or used as a complete meal replacement.

Smoothies are:

- Convenient and portable and can be taken anywhere
- Enjoyed by just about everyone, including children
- A quick and easy way to impress—and nourish—family and friends

Remember, the primary purpose of this book is to help you lose weight by making and drinking healthy smoothies, but drinking smoothies contributes to other aspects of your health as well.

SMOOTHIES AND YOUR HEALTH

As you'll learn in detail in Chapter 2, smoothies can help you lose weight. But what are the other health benefits that come with drinking a delicious, nutritious smoothie?

Smoothies offer a myriad of health benefits, especially when you consume them instead of higher-calorie, less-nutritious foods.

As demonstrated by the recipes in this book, smoothies offer a lot of diversity in flavor and nutritional content.

The majority of ingredients in smoothies are whole foods: foods in which the dietary fiber is left intact and is therefore retained in the liquid (unlike with juicing).

What exactly is fiber? Fiber is an indigestible carbohydrate that plays a big role in keeping the body healthy. There are two types of fiber:

1. Soluble (in water)
2. Insoluble (in water)

Both kinds help prevent disease by ridding the body of waste and dangerous toxic materials. Luckily, most plant-based foods contain both types of fiber; some are higher in soluble fiber, others in insoluble fiber. Smoothies are an excellent source of both types.

Soluble fiber can:

- Lower cholesterol
- Stabilize blood sugar levels

Insoluble fiber can:

- Relieve constipation
- Decrease the risk of type 2 diabetes

A diet high in fiber can also contribute to colon health, reduce blood pressure, and help with inflammation (a precursor to many types of disease).

The healthy smoothies in this book are also an excellent source of the micronutrients your body needs to be healthy. Micronutrients (better known as vitamins and minerals) are only necessary in small amounts, but deficiencies can result in serious health complications. These nutrients are crucial for the proper functioning of every organ in your body.

Eating a wide variety of foods, especially fruits and vegetables, takes care of your micronutrient needs. A good rule of thumb is to choose foods that differ in color (try to eat all the colors of the rainbow) and to drink smoothies that are nutritionally diverse.

Completing the picture are antioxidants, which are abundant in smoothie ingredients and which help prevent disease, including heart disease and cancer. Antioxidants fight off the free radicals (a type of highly charged molecule) that are linked to these and other types of chronic illness.

INGREDIENTS THAT CAN HELP YOU LOSE WEIGHT

Smoothies can be used for weight *gain* as well as weight loss. The key to achieving your goal is to choose the right ingredients, and the recipes in this book are designed with just that in mind. But when you decide to venture beyond these recipes, it's good to know which ingredients are beneficial for weight loss and which can be detrimental.

Chapter 2 will examine how the ingredients you choose can help or hinder your weight-loss program. For now, here are a couple of handy lists you can refer to. (In a nutshell, you want to use lower-calorie, higher-nutrient foods rather than higher-calorie, lower-nutrient foods.)

Beneficial Smoothie Ingredients for Weight Loss

- Coconut water (unsweetened)
- Flaxseed, chia seeds, hemp seeds
- Greens and vegetables
- Herbs and spices
- Low-fat milk
- Low-fat tofu
- Low-fat yogurt (regular or soy)
- Medjool dates (a natural sweetener that provides only 22 calories per date)*
- Oatmeal
- Plant-based milks (such as soy and almond, unsweetened)
- Skim milk

*Soak dates in water for easier use.

The ingredients listed here vary in the benefits they provide, but these benefits cover a wide spectrum of taste and nutrition.

Detrimental Smoothie Ingredients That Inhibit Weight Loss

- Avocados
- Coconut milk
- Nut butters
- Whole milk

The ingredients on the second list can sabotage your ability to lose weight because they're high in calories and fat. They are best avoided until you reach your weight-loss goals.

HOW TO MAKE A SMOOTHIE

Making a smoothie is easy:

1. Select a recipe.
2. Put the ingredients in your blender.
3. Blend and enjoy!

The reward is a refreshing chilled beverage full of your favorite foods and all the nutrients in them. Individual recipes will vary in detail, but rest assured, if you can follow these simple steps, you can make a smoothie!

TEN TIPS FOR MAKING GREAT SMOOTHIES

There's making a smoothie and then there's making a *great* smoothie. The latter is something of an acquired skill. These ten tips will help you maximize your smoothie-making potential:

1. Use frozen, ripe bananas.
2. Chill your glass or mug.
3. Buy seasonal fresh fruits.
4. Buy organic if possible.
5. Add the liquid ingredient(s) first.
6. Begin the blending process by using the lowest blender speed.
7. Blend thoroughly.
8. When measuring liquids, use recipes only as a guideline.
9. Have a good-quality blender.
10. Make extra and share.

A little elaboration:

1. For recipes that include bananas, frozen ripe bananas are the key to a creamier, milkshake-like result. Simply peel the banana, break it into two (or more) pieces, and then freeze it in a freezer-safe container. After a short time, the frozen banana will become the foundation for a cool, creamy treat.

2. What's better than a frosty treat in a frosty glass or mug? Aesthetics are important to any meal, and smoothies are no exception. Temperature is crucial, too. Adjust the time you chill your favorite smoothie glass in the refrigerator or freezer to your personal preference.

3. When using fresh fruit, try to buy what's in season in your part of the country. Not only will the fruit be fresher, but buying seasonally also helps reduce the negative effects that transporting foods long distances has on the environment.

4. Buying organic ingredients may not be possible due to lack of availability or cost. Purchase them when you can to avoid extra chemicals and pesticides in your smoothies.

5. Adding the liquid ingredients first makes the blending process work more efficiently. Food on the bottom (especially frozen fruit) may not budge without being in a liquid

6. Begin the blending process on the lowest speed. Then work your way slowly through the higher settings.

7. A great smoothie can be ruined if it is chunky instead of smooth. Don't make this mistake by rushing through the blending process.

8. The amount of liquid called for in a recipe is best used as a guideline until you're an experienced smoothie maker. You may prefer slightly different textures and thicknesses, so once you're comfortable making smoothies, feel free to adjust the amount of liquid to your liking. It's always best to start with a little less than the recommended amount (you can always add more).

9. You don't need a high-end, expensive blender. But do use one that is made by a good manufacturer and has a range of speeds.

10. Sharing smoothies only adds to the fun. Make extra and give some to a friend or weight-loss partner.

Losing Weight with the Smoothie Diet

The healthful smoothies in this book are so tasty and satisfying that you may be wondering whether they're too good to be true. Is drinking smoothies *really* an effective approach to losing weight? The answer is yes, for a number of reasons:

- **Control:** Drinking smoothies puts you in control of your own personal weight-loss program.
- **Low calories:** The recipes in this book use whole fruits and vegetables, which means they're naturally low in calories.
- **Variety:** Many dieting obstacles stem from a lack of interest in the foods dieters subject themselves to day after day. A good repertoire of smoothies offers the variety that can help you stick to a plan and successfully lose weight.

Healthful smoothies also contain the macronutrients and micronutrients that are essential for a healthy body. Smoothies are therefore an ideal replacement for meals containing foods that are higher in calories but contain fewer nutrients. These nutrients play a key role in losing weight.

HOW NUTRIENT-DENSE SMOOTHIES CAN HELP YOU LOSE WEIGHT

Macronutrients

The three primary macronutrients (nutrients we need in large amounts) that the smoothies in this book contain are:

1. Proteins
2. Carbohydrates
3. Fats

Protein

Protein facilitates weight loss via something called the thermic effect of food (TEF). TEF is the amount of energy (calories) the body uses to digest, absorb, and pass a given food as waste. Your body burns somewhere between 20 percent and 35 percent of the protein's calories during this process, making it an ideal nutrient for weight loss. For smoothies with the highest protein content, see Chapter 11.

Carbohydrates

All the smoothies in this book contain good amounts of carbohydrates, which are found in the fruits and vegetables that are the foundation of every recipe.

Carbohydrates are a key player in losing weight. This may seem confusing, as carbohydrates are often blamed for weight gain, not weight loss. But only *refined* carbohydrates are a concern when it comes to gaining weight. Refined carbohydrates are the ones that have been highly processed and contain no fiber (and no nutrients). A lack of fiber leads to a rapid rise in blood sugar, which tells the body to store fat—the exact opposite of what you're trying to achieve.

Fruits and vegetables contain natural, unprocessed, whole-food carbohydrates that still contain their original fiber. When you consume them, your blood sugar stays down, the body stores less fat, and the intact fiber keeps you feeling full and satisfied until your next meal (or smoothie). You won't overeat because you won't be hungry!

Here is how carbohydrates help with weight loss: Before they can be stored as fat, your body burns a certain number of calories (approximately 23) for every 100 calories of carbohydrates that you eat.

Fats

Fats are quite a different story. The only difference between dietary fat and body fat is approximately 3 calories per 100 calories consumed; in other words, your body only burns about 3 calories for every 100 calories of dietary fat that you eat before converting it into body fat. Fat also contains more than twice the number of calories per gram (9) than carbohydrates (4).

This information might make it seem like including *any* amount of fat in a smoothie designed for weight loss is out of the question. Certain foods high in fat and calories are definitely not a good idea and will sabotage weight loss (see the list of detrimental smoothie ingredients on page 5). However, a small amount of fat in the form of omega-3 fatty acids can be beneficial for losing weight as they are satiating and anti-inflammatory, and may:

- Increase blood flow to exercising muscles (which has a fat-burning effect)
- Facilitate the transportation of fat for energy storage (as opposed to fat storage)

Sources of omega-3 fatty acids in smoothies include:

- Chia seeds
- Flaxseeds
- Hemp seeds

Micronutrients

Feeling hungry is a real concern when you're trying to lose weight. This is where smoothies and their micronutrients (vitamins and minerals) come into play. Micronutrients alleviate hunger pangs and therefore overeating. When you start drinking smoothies, there may be a short period of time—a withdrawal phase—where you still feel hungry, but that will pass quickly if you stay committed to your weight-loss goals.

Exercise

Protein, carbohydrates, healthy fats, and micronutrients are crucial to your weight-loss program—and so is proper exercise. An effective exercise program will only enhance weight loss. Exercise speeds up the metabolism and contributes to overall weight loss.

There are three components to an effective exercise program:

1. Strength training
2. Cardiovascular training
3 Stretching and flexibility training

It's a common misconception that cardiovascular training trumps strength training when it comes to weight loss. Here is some information about the three components you should include in your exercise regimen:

1. Strength training may be the most important exercise component for losing weight due to its muscle-building effects. This type of exercise includes lifting weights or using your own body weight. Muscles require calories to function, so the more muscle tissue you have, the more calories you burn, allowing you to eat more and weigh less. Protein intake is important as it helps to rebuild muscle, grow tissue, and aid in recovery. Men and women alike will find positive results from strength training. And women don't need to be concerned about bulking up; due to the limited levels of testosterone in their bodies, strength training will only make women leaner, tighter, and smaller.
2. Cardiovascular training can encompass a variety of exercises, including running, aerobics, biking, swimming, and elliptical training. This type of training increases your lung capacity, increases blood circulation, lowers your resting heart rate, and burns fat and calories.
3. Stretching and flexibility training allow you to engage in other types of exercise more comfortably and therefore more effectively. Increased flexibility also results in faster recovery times when you perform other types of exercise. This leads to less downtime between workouts and hence more calorie burning and weight loss.

TEN TIPS FOR MOTIVATION AND SUCCESS

Motivation is an integral part of losing weight through healthful smoothies. The most successful outcomes are the result of planning and preparation (this is addressed in Chapter 4). The following tips will keep you going on days when you feel like you need a little extra help, and can make the difference between success and failure:

1. **Set goals.** The importance of *setting* goals cannot be underestimated when it comes to achieving goals. The most successful people set goals. Setting small, achievable goals will keep you focused and on track.
2. **Reward yourself for reaching these goals.** Rewards can be anything *but* food.
3. **Mix it up.** Variety is the spice of life. Make a variety of smoothies, not just a few. Boredom can slow your progress.
4. **Get a partner.** Having a weight-loss partner means you have someone to share your struggles as well as your successes with. An encouraging word always helps.

5. **Associate mealtime with calmness.** Whether you're eating a meal or drinking a smoothie, it's important to do so in a calm environment. Too much activity can hinder digestion.

6. **Relax.** Relax and don't stress it! Stress causes the body to release the hormone cortisol, which leads to belly fat accumulation.

7. **Don't skip meals.** Missing a meal may save a few calories, but it may also slow down your metabolism and lead to more unwanted pounds.

8. **Don't let yourself become famished.** Skipping meals will also leave you very hungry at the next meal. Compensating for missed calories only leads to overeating and weight gain.

9. **Engage in regular exercise.** Don't pass on exercise. If you need a reminder of the benefits of exercise, see page 11.

10. **Rest.** Inadequate rest is linked to overeating. A tired body can't function properly and tends to hold onto body fat.

MOST IMPORTANT: Don't feel guilty about taking care of yourself. You deserve it!

Three-Day Smoothie Detox

The buildup of toxins in the body is all too common in the lifestyle we lead today. Stress, heavy metals, allergens, medications, pollution, and, of course, food all contribute to this toxic load. Drinking healthful smoothies can help lighten this toxic load.

Toxins tend to accumulate in body fat, so ridding the body of excess fat is a crucial part of the detoxification process. Losing weight by drinking smoothies that are specifically geared for weight loss and detoxing is a good first step.

Certain micronutrients play a key role in ridding the body of these toxins. Some of these nutrients are vitamin C, the B vitamins, calcium, magnesium, selenium, manganese, copper, and zinc. The seventy-two smoothie recipes in this book have these nutrients in abundance.

Cruciferous vegetables (bok choy, broccoli, cabbage, cauliflower, collard greens, and kale) also increase the rate of detoxification. Most of these vegetables would not make a particularly good smoothie, but kale and broccoli actually do, and they're included in several recipes.

This leads us to the nine smoothies that are ideal for a three-day smoothie detox. One smoothie three times a day can jump-start your weight-loss plan or just boost your overall health.

NINE SMOOTHIES FOR A THREE-DAY DETOX*

Any of the smoothies in this book will help detoxify the body; however, the smoothies in Chapter 6 are specifically designed to maximize this effect. If you find that you're struggling with hunger while following this detox plan, simply drink an additional smoothie from Chapter 6 or any other chapter in this book.

Day 1

BREAKFAST BERRY-CUCUMBER SMOOTHIE

LUNCH HONEYDEW AND GREEN TEA SMOOTHIE

DINNER VERSATILE SMOOTHIE

Day 2

BREAKFAST BERRY-KALE SMOOTHIE

LUNCH PEACHY AND VANILLA SMOOTHIE

DINNER "IT'S ALL IN THERE" SMOOTHIE

Day 3

BREAKFAST BERRY-BEETY SMOOTHIE

LUNCH BROCCOLI POWER

DINNER GINGER AND PINEAPPLE SMOOTHIE

*When you are detoxing, use as much organic food as possible to avoid the pesticides and chemicals in conventional produce.

CHAPTER 4

Ten-Day Smoothie Meal Plan

Preparation is the key to success in any endeavor, and it's no different when drinking smoothies to lose weight.

Meal planning is what will give you the best results because it eliminates the need to think about what you're going to eat next—you already know. This approach limits overeating and falling off the weight-loss wagon. Planning your meals ahead of time also ensures that you will eat a variety of foods, not the same thing night after night. Meal planning is cost-effective too. A shopping list helps to limit waste and compare the prices of similar items.

For your convenience and as a teaching tool, this chapter lays out a ten-day smoothie meal plan. Here are some guidelines for future meal planning:

- Set a time to plan meals.
- Use a calendar or notebook to plan meals and schedule a shopping day.
- Choose the types of meals you want to serve (e.g. Mexican, casserole).
- Search for recipes if necessary.
- Make a shopping list.
- Start a meal journal.

The ten-day smoothie meal plan at the end of this chapter revolves around drinking two smoothies each day, one for breakfast and one for lunch. Dinner consists of a healthy, low-calorie, low-fat meal.

When planning meals for ten days, it's imperative to select a variety of smoothies from different categories to ensure that you consume an array of nutrients and enough calories. Here is a list of the twenty smoothies in the ten-day meal plan that follows:

1. Almond-Vanilla Breeze
2. Carrot Juice Smoothie

3   Chocolaty and Fruity Smoothie
4   Nectarine Surprise
5. Berry-Kale Smoothie
6. Honeydew and Green Tea Smoothie
7. "It's All in There" Smoothie
8. Fresh Papaya–Green Smoothie
9. Banana-Berry-Açai Smoothie
10. Berry, Oat, and Ginger Smoothie
11. Figgy Pudding Smoothie
12 It's a Fresh, Not Frozen Smoothie
13. Sweet Potato Smoothie
14. Sweet Berry–Pomegranate Smoothie
15. Banana-Oat Smoothie
16. Chocolaty Bean Smoothie
17. Quinoa-Banana Smoothie
18. Apple-Mango Spice Smoothie
19. Blackberry Cream Smoothie
20. Pumpkin Fall Smoothie

TEN DINNER SUGGESTIONS

1. **Mexican Night:** Two bean burritos (1 cup black beans, 2 corn tortillas, lettuce, tomatoes, salsa), 1 cup brown rice, lightly steamed greens
2. **Italian Night:** 4 to 6 ounces whole-grain pasta, ⅓ cup marinara sauce, 1 cup steamed broccoli, green salad
3. **Veggie Wraps:** 2 brown rice wraps loaded with steamed veggies (mushrooms, peppers, onions), lightly steamed greens
4. **Stir-Fry:** 6 ounces rice noodles, crispy tofu, steamed veggies, soy sauce
5. **Salad as a Meal:** large green salad, 1 cup beans, raw veggies of choice, low-fat dressing
6. **Breakfast for Dinner:** 1 cup steel-cut oatmeal topped with cinnamon and vanilla, 1 cup fruit, 2 slices dry whole-grain toast
7. **Beans and Rice:** 1 cup brown rice, 1 cup beans, lightly steamed greens
8. **Soup:** 1 cup beans, veggies, seasonings
9. **Stuffed Squash (or pepper):** 1 cup whole-grain rice, steamed veggies, seasonings

10. **Beans and Greens:** 1 cup whole-grain rice, 1 cup beans, lightly steamed kale and collard greens

These smoothies and dinner suggestions are practical and easy to make. They can be combined in any number of ways.

The following is just one example of what you can do with these selections. Feel free to pick your own smoothies—just keep in mind the best approach is to select smoothies from a variety of categories.

Day 1

BREAKFAST ALMOND-VANILLA BREEZE

LUNCH PUMPKIN FALL SMOOTHIE

DINNER MEXICAN NIGHT

Day 2

BREAKFAST CARROT JUICE SMOOTHIE

LUNCH BLACKBERRY CREAM SMOOTHIE

DINNER ITALIAN NIGHT

Day 3

BREAKFAST CHOCOLATY AND FRUITY SMOOTHIE

LUNCH APPLE-MANGO SPICE SMOOTHIE

DINNER VEGGIE WRAPS

Day 4

BREAKFAST NECTARINE SURPRISE

LUNCH QUINOA-BANANA SMOOTHIE

DINNER STIR-FRY

Day 5

BREAKFAST BERRY-KALE SMOOTHIE

LUNCH CHOCOLATY BEAN SMOOTHIE

DINNER SALAD AS A MEAL

Day 6

BREAKFAST BERRY, OAT, AND GINGER SMOOTHIE

LUNCH HONEYDEW AND GREEN TEA SMOOTHIE

DINNER BREAKFAST FOR DINNER

Day 7

BREAKFAST SWEET BERRY-POMEGRANATE SMOOTHIE

LUNCH "IT'S ALL IN THERE" SMOOTHIE

DINNER BEANS AND RICE

Day 8

BREAKFAST IT'S A FRESH, NOT FROZEN SMOOTHIE

LUNCH BANANA-OAT SMOOTHIE

DINNER SOUP

Day 9

BREAKFAST: FIGGY PUDDING SMOOTHIE

LUNCH: FRESH PAPAYA–GREEN SMOOTHIE

DINNER: STUFFED SQUASH

Day 10

BREAKFAST: BANANA-BERRY-AÇAI SMOOTHIE

LUNCH: SWEET POTATO SMOOTHIE

DINNER: BEANS AND GREENS

CHAPTER 5

Breakfast Smoothies

Almond-Vanilla Breeze

The taste of real almonds without all the fat makes this smooth and creamy drink a breakfast to look forward to. The milk and fruit supply a multitude of nutrients, including calcium and vitamins D and E, making it a healthful breakfast too.

½ CUP UNSWEETENED VANILLA ALMOND MILK

½ CUP ORANGE JUICE

½ FROZEN BANANA

½ CUP FRESH OR FROZEN PINEAPPLE CHUNKS

1 CUP FROZEN MANGO

½ CUP FROZEN BLUEBERRIES

In a blender, combine all ingredients and blend until smooth.

Carrot Juice Smoothie

Once you've had freshly juiced carrots and apples, it's hard to drink any other kind. The same goes for drinking freshly made smoothies. While carrot and apple juice alone are nutritious and delicious, they lack fiber. Bananas pick up the slack and bring substance to this orange breakfast drink.

1 CUP FRESH CARROT JUICE

½ CUP FRESH APPLE JUICE

2 FROZEN BANANAS

In a blender combine all ingredients and blend until the smoothie is a pleasing color.

Chia for Breakfast Smoothie

It might be surprising to learn that the teeny-tiny chia seeds in this breakfast smoothie add tons of nutrition, including calcium, phosphorus, manganese, and the anti-inflammatory omega-3 fatty acids (healthy fats) discussed in Chapter 2. That's a lot of goodness to take in for breakfast!

1 RED DELICIOUS APPLE, CORED, PEELED, AND CHOPPED

½ CUP COCONUT WATER

1 CARROT, PEELED AND CHOPPED

¼-INCH PIECE FRESH GINGER ROOT, PEELED

1 TABLESPOON CHIA SEEDS

In a blender, combine apple and coconut water and blend for 15 seconds. Add the carrot and blend for another 15 seconds. Add the ginger and chia seeds and blend until smooth.

Chocolaty and Fruity Smoothie

Who doesn't love chocolate? At 10 calories per tablespoon, add as much cacao powder as you'd like to this smoothie. A source of iron and dietary fiber, it's actually good for you!

1 CUP LOW-FAT REGULAR OR SOY MILK

1 FROZEN BANANA

½ CUP FROZEN PINEAPPLE CHUNKS

2 FROZEN STRAWBERRIES

½ TABLESPOON UNSWEETENED NATURAL COCOA POWDER

In a blender, combine milk, fruit, and cacao powder, and blend until smooth. Add water if desired.

Mango–Carrot Juice Smoothie

A little mango and carrot juice will get you going in the morning. Both fruits are full of healthy carbohydrates and have a powerful, sweet taste you'll look forward to; this will help you rise early and embrace what the day has to offer. A little nutmeg spices up this smoothie in more ways than one: Nutmeg has been credited with stimulating brain function and even contains a natural compound known to help prevent Alzheimer's disease.

1½ CUPS FROZEN MANGO
½ CUP CARROT JUICE
PINCH OF NUTMEG

In a blender, combine all ingredients and blend until smooth.

Nectarine Surprise

Nectarines are a surprising source of beta-carotene (the precursor to vitamin A in the body) and contain numerous other vitamins and minerals you need to get your day off to a good start. Full of fiber, nectarines will provide you with a stable blood-sugar level and the energy you need to keep going until lunchtime rolls around.

1 FROZEN BANANA
3 NECTARINES, PEELED AND PITTED
2 MEDJOOL DATES
¾ CUP UNSWEETENED LOW-FAT REGULAR OR SOY MILK
1 TEASPOON VANILLA EXTRACT
⅛ TEASPOON CINNAMON

In a blender, combine all ingredients and blend until smooth and creamy.

New Zealand Smoothie

New Zealand would be proud of this smoothie. The country exports kiwi, the star of this drink, and is the home of the kiwi bird, which is also New Zealand's national symbol. In addition to its sweet flavor, kiwi provides more vitamin C than orange juice, so blend away!

2 KIWIS, PEELED AND CUT INTO CHUNKS
1 FROZEN BANANA
½ CUP FROZEN BLUEBERRIES
2 MEDJOOL DATES
1½ CUPS CRUSHED ICE
½ CUP LOW-FAT YOGURT (REGULAR OR SOY)
⅛ TEASPOON ALMOND EXTRACT (OPTIONAL)

In a blender, combine all ingredients and blend thoroughly. Add the almond extract if you'd like an extra kick!

Red Grape Smoothie

An unusual blend of grapes, strawberries, and bananas makes this a breakfast packed with potassium, vitamins C and K, manganese, vitamin B6, and antioxidants. The grapes add a lot of water to this breakfast smoothie, making any other liquid unnecessary, but you can add water if desired.

1 CUP RED SEEDLESS GRAPES
1 CUP FROZEN STRAWBERRIES
1 BANANA
WATER (OPTIONAL)

In a blender, combine all ingredients and blend until smooth. Add water if desired.

Spinach-Mango Salad

Do you feel stressed first thing in the morning? Relax with this salad in a glass. Fresh baby spinach not only contains antioxidants, vitamins, minerals, and fiber, but can also have a beneficial effect on your blood pressure.

4 CUPS ROMAINE LETTUCE, CHOPPED
½ CUP LOW-FAT REGULAR OR SOY MILK
1 CUP FRESH BABY SPINACH
1 CUP FROZEN MANGO

In a blender, combine lettuce with milk and blend in small batches, a bit at a time. Add spinach and mango and finish blending until smooth.

CHAPTER 6

Cleansing Smoothies

Berry-Beety Smoothie

Beets may not be an everyday smoothie ingredient, but they should be! They're a great source of betalains, phytonutrients that are not only anti-inflammatory and powerful antioxidants, but also assist the body in detoxifying.

½ CUP COOKED, PEELED, AND CHOPPED BEETS, CHILLED
½ CUP FROZEN RASPBERRIES
¼ CUP CRANBERRY JUICE, CHILLED IF DESIRED
½ CUP LOW-FAT YOGURT (REGULAR OR SOY)
FRESH RASPBERRIES (OPTIONAL)

In a blender, combine all ingredients and blend until smooth. Add fresh raspberries on top for added taste and nutrition if desired.

Berry-Cucumber Smoothie

Cucumbers bring flavonoids, lignans, and triterpenes to this smoothie, but all you really need to know is that cucumbers are a refreshing way to cleanse the body. Composed largely of water, they have the capacity to restore bodily fluids to healthy levels.

2 FROZEN BANANAS
½ CUP FROZEN STRAWBERRIES
½ CUCUMBER, PEELED
½ CUP FROZEN PINEAPPLE
½ CUP WATER

In a blender, combine all ingredients and blend until smooth.

Berry-Kale Smoothie

Berries and kale make for a great combination and are key components of any weight-loss plan. Low in calories, high in nutrition, and virtually fat free, this smoothie is delicious and good for detoxing too!

¼ CUP FROZEN BLUEBERRIES

¼ CUP FROZEN RASPBERRIES

¼ CUP FROZEN STRAWBERRIES

2 KALE LEAVES, WASHED AND STEMMED

½ CUP WATER

In a blender, combine all ingredients and blend until smooth.

Broccoli Power

Cruciferous foods are effective detoxifiers. The phytonutrients in broccoli maximize the detox effect for optimal cleansing.

2 BANANAS, 1 FROZEN AND 1 AT ROOM TEMPERATURE

1 CUP FROZEN BROCCOLI

1 CUP BABY KALE

1 CUP WATER

In a blender, combine all ingredients and blend until smooth.

Ginger and Pineapple Smoothie

Ginger is used in a variety of foods, and now you can add smoothies to that list too. Pain, inflammation, and common respiratory problems are reduced by this healing root. Ginger may even rev up the metabolism for maximum weight loss.

⅛ TEASPOON PEELED, GRATED GINGER ROOT

1 CUP APPLE JUICE

½ APPLE

½ CUP FROZEN PINEAPPLE

1 CUP ICE

In a blender, combine ginger and apple juice and blend for 15 seconds. Add the apple, pineapple, and ice, and blend until smooth.

Honeydew and Green Tea Smoothie

Honeydew melon and green tea come together to create a powerhouse of anti-oxidants and B vitamins for a detox effect. Naturally low in calories and full of water, honeydew is ideal for weight loss and cleansing.

1 FROZEN BANANA

¾ CUP HONEYDEW MELON, CUT INTO CHUNKS

¾ CUP STRONG BREWED GREEN TEA

2 MEDJOOL DATES

¼ CUP REGULAR OR ALMOND MILK

In a blender, combine all ingredients and blend until smooth.

"It's All in There" Smoothie

From vitamin C to zinc, the ingredients in this recipe provide the micronutrients needed to cleanse the body and facilitate weight loss.

¾ CUP LOW-FAT REGULAR OR ALMOND MILK

½ CUP FRESHLY SQUEEZED ORANGE JUICE

1 FROZEN BANANA

¼ CUP FROZEN PINEAPPLE

½ CUP MANGO

2 KALE LEAVES, STEMMED AND CHOPPED

½ CUP FROZEN BLUEBERRIES

1 TABLESPOON GOLDEN FLAXSEED MEAL

In a blender, combine milk and orange juice. Add remaining ingredients and blend until smooth.

Peachy and Vanilla Smoothie

Because oat bran is so high in soluble fiber, it has a cleansing effect on the body. Moving toxins and debris out of the body via the gastrointestinal (GI) tract leads to healthy bowel movements and enhanced digestion.

1 TABLESPOON OAT BRAN

½ CUP LOW-FAT REGULAR OR ALMOND MILK

½ CUP FROZEN PEACHES

1 FROZEN BANANA

⅛ TEASPOON VANILLA EXTRACT

1 TABLESPOON MAPLE SYRUP

1 CUP ICE

In a small bowl, soak the oat bran in the milk for a few minutes. In a blender, combine oat bran–milk mixture with remaining ingredients and blend until smooth.

Versatile Smoothie

The beauty of this smoothie is its ability to be green, aid digestion, and assist in detoxing the body—all at the same time. The green part is packed with health, the pineapple and ginger are friendly to your digestive tract, and the kale helps flush toxins from the body. It's a win-win-win situation!

3 ROMAINE LETTUCE LEAVES, CHOPPED

2 KALE LEAVES, STEMMED AND CHOPPED

¼ CUP CHOPPED FRESH PARSLEY

¼ CUP CHOPPED FRESH PINEAPPLE

¼ CUP CHOPPED FRESH MANGO

½-INCH PIECE FRESH GINGER ROOT, PEELED AND CHOPPED

¾ CUPS WATER

In a blender, combine all ingredients and blend until smooth.

Green Smoothies

Apricot-Green Smoothie

Native to China, apricots are now grown worldwide. In the United States, they are grown in California and, on a smaller scale, Virginia. Nutrient-rich, their flavor is somewhere between that of a plum and a peach.

6 APRICOTS
2 APPLES, CORED AND CHOPPED
1 CUP STRAWBERRIES
2 CUPS CHOPPED FRESH SPINACH
2 CARROTS, CHOPPED
1 CUP WATER

In a blender, combine all ingredients and blend until smooth.

Beet Green Smoothie

While it's not safe to juice beet greens, because of their high oxalic acid content, it's perfectly okay to blend them. Beet greens are a powerhouse of nutrients and supply the body with vitamins A, B, C, E, and K, as well as calcium, iron, copper, magnesium, manganese, potassium, and sodium.

1 APPLE, CORED, PEELED, AND CHOPPED
1 BANANA
1 CUP STRAWBERRIES
2 CUPS CHOPPED BEET GREENS
½ CUP WATER

In a blender, combine all ingredients and blend until smooth, adding more water as needed.

Free-for-All Green Smoothie

For this smoothie, feel free to mix it up a little. Change one or more ingredients to suit your preference and vary the smoothie's taste and nutritional content. Try milk or juice instead of water, kale or chard instead spinach, mango or peaches instead of banana, or berries instead of apples.

1 CUP WATER

1 CUP SPINACH

1 BANANA

2 APPLES, CORED, PEELED, AND CHOPPED

In a blender, combine all ingredients and blend until smooth.

Fresh Papaya–Green Smoothie

Fresh fruit makes this green smoothie extra inviting—and extra tasty. Papaya is the star. Credited with providing protection against rheumatoid arthritis and prostate cancer, this tropical fruit is a welcome addition to any green smoothie.

1 CUP PAPAYA CHUNKS

1 CUP PINEAPPLE CHUNKS

2 TANGERINES, PEELED, SEEDED, AND CHOPPED

2 CUPS CHOPPED BEET GREENS

1 STALK CELERY

¾ CUP WATER

In a blender, combine all ingredients and blend until smooth.

Green and Lean Smoothie

You'll feel green and lean when you imbibe this concoction infused with tangerine and mint. Supplying a variety of vitamins and minerals (and low in calories), this one is a sure winner in the fight against flab! (Use freshly squeezed tangerine juice for an added flavor boost.)

1 CUP BABY SPINACH

1 CUP CUCUMBER CHUNKS

1 KIWI, PEELED AND CUT INTO CHUNKS

½ CUP NONFAT VANILLA YOGURT (REGULAR OR SOY)

½ CUP TANGERINE JUICE

¼ CUP MINT LEAVES, PLUS MORE FOR GARNISH

In a blender, combine all ingredients and blend until smooth. Add mint leaves for garnish if desired.

Italian Parsley and Mint Smoothie

As healthy as this smoothie is—and as good as it tastes—pregnant women should not drink it; apiol, an essential oil contained in parsley, may lead to uterine contractions. But for everyone else, these greens are safe and nutritious. Parsley provides 150 percent of the recommended daily value of vitamin K, and mint has a cleansing effect in the body.

2 CUPS SEEDLESS WATERMELON CHUNKS

1 FRESH MINT LEAF, CHOPPED

1 CUP STRAWBERRIES

1 CUP CHOPPED FRESH ITALIAN PARSLEY

Put the watermelon in the bottom of a blender and add remaining ingredients. Blend until smooth.

It's Easy Being Green

It's easy being green when you drink this smoothie. Boston Bibb lettuce, a.k.a. butter lettuce, is a special treat due to its unique flavor and texture. It delivers not only great taste, but also vitamins A and K along with potassium and folate.

¼ CUP FRESH SPINACH

¼ CUP BOSTON BIBB LETTUCE

2 KALE LEAVES, STEMMED

1 CUP FROZEN PINEAPPLE

3 KIWIS, PEELED AND CUT INTO CHUNKS

1 FROZEN BANANA

½ CUP WATER

In a blender, combine all ingredients and blend until green.

Plum Salad Smoothie

Juicy and sweet, plums come in a variety of colors. All varieties supply vitamins A, C, and K, as well as a good amount of dietary fiber and potassium. Plums are credited with aiding in the prevention of age-related macular degeneration (ARMD), a loss of vision that affects some people later in life.

¾ CUP LOW-FAT REGULAR OR ALMOND MILK

2 PLUMS, PITTED

½ CUP FRESH CRANBERRIES

2 BANANAS

1 HEAD ROMAINE LETTUCE

In a blender, combine milk and plums and pulse for 30 seconds. Add remaining ingredients and blend until smooth and creamy.

Raring-to-Go Green Smoothie

Red leaf lettuce is recognized as a calorie-free, fat-free food. Even so, it's a source of nutrients, including vitamins A and K and dietary fiber. These vitamins are responsible for good vision, helping the blood to clot properly, and maintaining bone density. Go green!

½ CUP WATER

1 KIWI, PEELED

½ CUP GREEN SEEDLESS GRAPES

½ ORANGE

1 ORANGE TOMATO

2 LEAVES RED LEAF LETTUCE

In a blender, combine kiwi and water. Add remaining ingredients and blend until smooth.

CHAPTER 8

Antioxidant Smoothies

Banana-Berry-Açai Smoothie

A staple of the Amazon peoples for centuries, the açai berry should be a staple of your diet too. This dark purple drupe contains a multitude of polyphenolic anthocyanin compounds (antioxidants) and may fight premature aging, inflammation, and even cancer. Although not proven conclusively, açai berries may even decrease your appetite!

1 OUNCE AÇAI BERRY JUICE
1 CUP FROZEN BLUEBERRIES
½ CUP FROZEN STRAWBERRIES
1 FROZEN BANANA
½ TO ¾ CUP WATER

In a blender, combine all ingredients and blend until smooth.

Açai Berry Juice Smoothie

This great smoothie contains the antioxidant power of açai berry juice. (Use it sparingly, though—it's strong and powerful!) The red grapes increase the amount of glutathione (an essential antioxidant nutrient) in the body and protect cell membranes from damage caused by cancer-causing molecules.

½ HEAD ROMAINE LETTUCE, CHOPPED
⅛ CUP WATER
1 OUNCE AÇAI BERRY JUICE
1 FROZEN BANANA
½ CUP RED GRAPES

In a blender, combine lettuce, water, and juice, and blend for 15 seconds. Add remaining ingredients and blend until smooth.

Berry Good Smoothie

If berries are your thing, this smoothie should be right up your alley! It's a creamy vanilla approach to health, wellness, and weight loss. Blackberries and raspberries are among the fruits with the lowest glycemic index (great for keeping your blood sugar down) and are powerful little packages of vitamins, antioxidants, and dietary fiber.

6 OUNCES VANILLA YOGURT (REGULAR OR SOY)

1 FROZEN BANANA

½ CUP BLACKBERRIES

1 CUP FRESH RASPBERRIES

2 MEDJOOL DATES

4 ICE CUBES

Put yogurt in a blender and blend until smooth, gradually adding the remaining ingredients and adding the ice cubes in the middle.

Berry, Oat, and Ginger Smoothie

Blueberries and oatmeal combine wonderfully together in a bowl, and this smoothie translates that combination to a glass. The oats provide a unique texture, and the blueberries provide more antioxidants than most other fruits and vegetables. Ginger is also one of the top five antioxidant foods.

⅛ CUP OLD-FASHIONED ROLLED OATS

½ CUP WATER

½ TEASPOON FRESHLY GRATED GINGER

1 CUP FROZEN BLUEBERRIES

½ CUP PLAIN LOW-FAT YOGURT (REGULAR OR SOY)

½ CUP ICE

4 MEDJOOL DATES

Soak the oats in the water for 10 to 15 minutes. In a blender, combine oats with ginger, then add remaining ingredients. Blend until frothy.

Berry-Peary Smoothie

A large proportion of a pear's nutritional value is contained in its skin. This includes the phenolic phytonutrients—its antioxidants, flavonoids, and cancer-fighting compounds. Keep in mind that it's a good idea to seek out organic foods when using skins.

¾ CUP LOW-FAT REGULAR OR ALMOND MILK

⅛ CUP RASPBERRIES

1½ ORGANIC RIPE PEARS, CORED

6 ICE CUBES

In a blender, combine all ingredients and blend. Pour into a chilled glass and enjoy!

Sweet Red Cherry–Açai Smoothie

This smoothie uses frozen açai purée, a convenient, easy way to make a potent antioxidant drink. Usually found in your grocer's frozen natural foods section, this purée packs just as many antioxidants as the whole berry. Throw in some antioxidant-rich dark sweet cherries and increase the benefits even more.

½ CUP COCONUT WATER

½ POUCH (3.5 OUNCES) FROZEN AÇAI PURÉE

½ CUP FROZEN DARK SWEET CHERRIES

1 FROZEN BANANA

In a blender, combine coconut water and purée. Blend for 30 seconds, then add remaining ingredients, and blend until smooth. Add more coconut water if needed.

Green Tomato Smoothie

The tomato in this smoothie isn't green (it's orange), but the drink is. Research shows that orange tomatoes lead to better absorption of lycopene, a carotenoid (antioxidant) associated with a decreased risk of prostate cancer.

1 BANANA

1 CUP STRAWBERRIES

2 CUPS FRESH BABY SPINACH

1 ORANGE TOMATO, CHOPPED

Add water to a blender, then add remaining ingredients. Blend until green.

Pomegranate, Anyone?

Fuel your day with the power of pomegranates! A great source of vitamin C, potassium, dietary fiber, and several polyphenols (antioxidants), you can't go wrong when it comes to anything with pomegranates (or their juice).

1 CUP POMEGRANATE JUICE

¾ CUP LOW-FAT REGULAR OR ALMOND MILK

1 FROZEN BANANA

¼ TEASPOON ALMOND EXTRACT

2 MEDJOOL DATES

ICE CUBES (OPTIONAL)

In a blender, combine all ingredients and blend until smooth. Add ice cubes if desired for an even more refreshing beverage.

Sweet and Creamy Pineapple Smoothie

Who doesn't love a creamy pineapple drink? Loaded with vitamin C and manganese, this sweet smoothie brings to mind warm, breezy days lounging on a tropical beach. The fun is as close as your blender! Use frozen pineapple for an even creamier smoothie.

1 CUP FRESH OR FROZEN PINEAPPLE, CUT INTO CHUNKS

¼ CUP LOW-FAT REGULAR OR SOY MILK

¼ CUP LOW-FAT VANILLA YOGURT (REGULAR OR SOY)

2 MEDJOOL DATES

In a blender, combine all ingredients and blend until very smooth. Enjoy!

Low-Fat Smoothies

Apple Cider Smoothie

Apple cider is a more fresh and nutritious alternative to apple juice. Unpasteurized and unfiltered, cider retains the sediment and pulp of the original fruit, which is where the fiber is, along with much of the nutrition, including potassium. Farmers' markets are a great place to buy fresh, inexpensive apple cider. Use it just like any other liquid for a great smoothie.

⅔ CUP APPLE CIDER

½ CUP FROZEN PEACHES

¼ CUP FROZEN STRAWBERRIES

1 FROZEN BANANA

¼ TEASPOON CINNAMON

In a blender, combine all ingredients and blend until smooth.

Vitamin C Smorgasbord

Did you know that vitamin C is crucial for healthy weight loss? Research shows that the less vitamin C you take in, the more likely you are to be overweight, especially around the midsection. Vitamin C helps your body break down the stored body fat you're trying so hard to lose. This smoothie is designed with just that in mind, as every ingredient here is loaded with vitamin C!

1 ORANGE, PEELED AND SEEDED

¼ CANTALOUPE, SLICED

½ CUP STRAWBERRIES

½ TOMATO, CHOPPED

In a blender, combine all ingredients and blend until smooth.

Canned Fruit Smoothie

Smoothies can be made with fresh, frozen, or even canned fruit. The key is to use canned fruit naturals—in other words, fruit in its own juice, not sweetened syrup. Even though canned fruit contains no fat, using the natural versions significantly cuts down on calories and sugar, and thus the possibility of weight gain.

1½ CUPS CANNED PEACHES, DRAINED, WITH SOME JUICE RESERVED

1 FROZEN BANANA

½ CUP CANNED PINEAPPLE, DRAINED, WITH SOME JUICE RESERVED

¾ CUP UNSWEETENED VANILLA ALMOND MILK

2 MEDJOOL DATES

In a blender, combine all ingredients and blend until smooth. Add reserved canned fruit juice if desired.

Cherry-Kale Smoothie

Dark sweet cherries and kale combine to make an almost chocolaty smoothie that will satisfy your sweet tooth, your intake of cruciferous vegetables, and your low-fat needs. Better yet, the cinnamon in this recipe stabilizes your blood sugar and leads to less fat storage.

2 KALE LEAVES, STEMMED AND CHOPPED

½ CUP WATER

1 CUP FROZEN DARK SWEET CHERRIES

1 FROZEN BANANA

¼ TEASPOON VANILLA EXTRACT

¼ TEASPOON CINNAMON

In a blender, combine kale and water. Add remaining ingredients and blend until smooth.

Cranberry Smoothie

Red, tart berries, cranberries supply vitamin C, vitamin B6, dietary fiber, and manganese, which are all important components of any healthy weight-loss program. Cranberries are also low in calories and fat. Combined with low-fat or skim milk, they make this smoothie an excellent choice when looking for a low-fat beverage.

½ CUP FROZEN CRANBERRIES

1 RIPE BANANA

1 CUP SKIM REGULAR OR ALMOND MILK

2 MEDJOOL DATES

CRANBERRY JUICE (OPTIONAL)

In a blender, combine all ingredients and blend until smooth. Add a splash of cranberry juice, if desired, for a little extra flavor.

Creamy Coconut–Mango Smoothie

Your taste buds will get excited just reading about this combination of flavors. The mango and orange juice offer up plenty of vitamin A and C, and the coconuty taste doesn't disappoint.

½ CUP COCONUT WATER, CHILLED

1 CUP LOW-FAT VANILLA YOGURT (REGULAR OR SOY)

1 CUP FROZEN OR FRESH MANGO

2 TABLESPOONS FROZEN ORANGE JUICE CONCENTRATE

In a blender, combine all ingredients and blend until smooth.

Orange Crush Smoothie

Antioxidants, vitamins (especially vitamin C), minerals, fiber, and great taste—without any fat! Maybe this smoothie isn't a real orange crush, but who needs one when you have this trio of flavors and an all-natural approach to losing weight?

2 ORANGES, PEELED, SEEDED, AND CUT INTO CHUNKS
½ CUP FROZEN RASPBERRIES
½ CUP FROZEN BLUEBERRIES
½ CUP ICE

In a blender, combine all ingredients and blend until smooth. Add water if desired.

Three-Ingredient Smoothie

Technically, this three-ingredient smoothie contains four ingredients when you add the water, but three sounds much more impressive! And impressive this smoothie is—especially when you consider the amount of nutrition that's packed into one banana, a cup of blueberries, and a cup of yogurt.

1 FROZEN BANANA
1 CUP FROZEN BLUEBERRIES
1 CUP LOW-FAT YOGURT (REGULAR OR SOY)

In a blender, combine all ingredients and blend until smooth. Add water if desired.

Vanilla Banana Freeze

Got (banana) milk? This simple smoothie turns frozen bananas into an unconventional milk complete with vanilla and cinnamon for a unique flavor twist. Using unsweetened almond milk makes it even more delicious.

1½ CUPS LOW-FAT REGULAR OR ALMOND MILK

2 FROZEN BANANAS

2 MEDJOOL DATES

½ TEASPOON VANILLA EXTRACT

GROUND CINNAMON (FOR GARNISH)

In a blender, combine all ingredients and blend until smooth. Add ground cinnamon if desired.

CHAPTER 10

High-Energy Smoothies

Original High-Energy Smoothie

This combination of antioxidant-rich foods will make you feel light and energized. Perfect before or after a strenuous workout, these foods will fuel both your exercise program and your recovery.

½ CUP FROZEN PINEAPPLE

½ CUP SEEDLESS WATERMELON

¼ CUP COCONUT WATER

1 HANDFUL BABY SPINACH

½ CUP FROZEN BLUEBERRIES

1 GREEN APPLE, PEELED, CORED, AND CHOPPED

In a blender, combine all the ingredients and blend until smooth.

Carrot-Kiwi Smoothie

This is a fun, light smoothie that can be enjoyed any time of day. It's an ideal antidote to the afternoon slump (and a much better choice than the candy bar that used to be in your desk). The carrots, apple, and kiwi provide the (natural) sugar you're looking for.

2 LARGE CARROTS, PEELED AND CHOPPED

1 APPLE, PEELED, CORED, AND CHOPPED

1 CUP APPLE JUICE

1 KIWI, PEELED

2 TABLESPOONS LOW-FAT YOGURT (REGULAR OR SOY)

FRESH BASIL LEAVES (OPTIONAL)

In a blender, combine carrots, apple, and apple juice and blend for 30 seconds. Add the remaining ingredients and blend until smooth. Add basil if desired.

Coconut, Pineapple, and Spinach Smoothie

Coconut water comes from young green coconuts and is used to replenish the electrolytes you need to stay hydrated and energized. This smoothie will give you a boost to get through the busy day.

½ CUP CHOPPED PINEAPPLE

½ CUP CHOPPED SEEDLESS WATERMELON

½ CUP COCONUT WATER

½ CUP BABY SPINACH

½ CUP FROZEN BLUEBERRIES

1 FROZEN BANANA

In a blender, combine all ingredients and blend until smooth.

Figgy Pudding Smoothie

In addition to being a high-energy food, figs provide iron, potassium, magnesium, vitamin K, and some B vitamins. They're the best source of calcium among fruit and are also a good source of dietary fiber.

10 FRESH BLACK FIGS

½ CUP LOW-FAT VANILLA YOGURT (REGULAR OR SOY)

½ CUP VANILLA SOY MILK

1 TABLESPOON GOLDEN FLAXSEED MEAL

½ TEASPOON GROUND CINNAMON

Soak figs in water for a few minutes; drain. In a blender, combine figs with yogurt and milk and blend for 30 seconds. Add flaxseed and cinnamon and blend until smooth. Add water if desired.

Guava Juice Smoothie

Grown in the tropics, guava is rich in vitamins and minerals and also facilitates energy production in cells. This smoothie will increase energy levels by fueling your daily activities, your muscles, and your mind.

2 CUPS CHOPPED SEEDLESS WATERMELON

½ CUP FROZEN STRAWBERRIES

½ CUP GUAVA JUICE

In a blender, combine all ingredients and blend until smooth.

It's a Fresh, Not Frozen Smoothie

Fresh and frozen fruits both make great smoothies, but this one's all fresh! Fresh orange juice delivers more vitamin C, enzymes, and flavor.

1 CUP FRESHLY SQUEEZED ORANGE JUICE

5 STRAWBERRIES

12 BLUEBERRIES

3 BLACKBERRIES

3 RASPBERRIES

1 FROZEN BANANA

1 MEDJOOL DATE

In a blender, combine all ingredients and blend until smooth.

Sweet Potato Smoothie

Sweet potatoes are a high-carbohydrate and therefore a high-energy food. But in a smoothie? These tubers are a welcome addition to any meal, including smoothies. But be sweet potato–savvy: Research shows steaming and boiling release more of the sweet potato's antioxidant and anti-inflammatory effects than baking.

½ LARGE SWEET POTATO, PEELED, COOKED, AND COOLED

½ CUP LOW-FAT REGULAR OR SOY MILK

½ BANANA

½ APPLE

DASH OF NUTMEG

½ TEASPOON VANILLA EXTRACT

1 CUP ICE

In a blender, combine all ingredients and blend until smooth.

Spicy Apple Cider Smoothie

If you're looking for a little extra oomph and energy, this smoothie is the right choice. The maple syrup provides a substantial amount of manganese, a trace mineral that the body uses to facilitate energy production in cells.

¾ CUP APPLE CIDER

¾ CUP ORANGE JUICE

1½ CUPS APPLESAUCE

1 TABLESPOON MAPLE SYRUP

¼ TEASPOON NUTMEG

¼ TEASPOON CINNAMON

In a blender, combine cider and juice. Add the applesauce, maple syrup, and spices and blend until smooth.

Sweet Berry–Pomegranate Smoothie

This smoothie is powered by pomegranate, and you will be too after you drain your glass. This red juicy fruit is an excellent source of iron and helps to prevent weakness and dizziness. The combined nutrient power of pomegranates also increases the amount of oxygen the heart is able to use, leading to a more energy-filled day.

1 CUP POMEGRANATE JUICE

1 CUP FRESH SPINACH, CHOPPED

1 CUP BOSTON BIBB LETTUCE, CHOPPED

¼ CUCUMBER, CHOPPED

½ CUP FROZEN BLUEBERRIES

1 CUP FROZEN STRAWBERRIES

3 MEDJOOL DATES

1 CUP ICE

In a blender, combine all ingredients and blend until smooth.

Protein Smoothies

Banana-Oat Smoothie

This protein smoothie provides all of the benefits associated with the warming taste of cinnamon. This spice has antioxidant, antimicrobial, and anticlotting properties and helps regulate blood sugar and improve brain function.

¼ CUP OLD-FASHIONED ROLLED OATS

¾ CUP PLAIN LOW-FAT YOGURT (REGULAR OR SOY)

½ FROZEN BANANA

¾ CUP SKIM MILK OR UNSWEETENED SOY MILK

2 MEDJOOL DATES

¼ TEASPOON GROUND CINNAMON

Soak the oats in water; drain. In a blender, combine oats with remaining ingredients and blend until smooth.

Berry Fruity Tofutti

Like having a fruit pie in a glass, this smoothie provides antioxidants, phyto-nutrients, and a sweet, inviting taste. The tofu packs this refreshing vegan libation with protein, calcium, and iron too.

1 CUP FROZEN MIXED BERRIES

½ CUP WHITE GRAPE JUICE

2 MEDJOOL DATES

1 FROZEN BANANA

½ PACKAGE (7 OUNCES) SILKEN TOFU, DRAINED AND RINSED

In a blender, combine all ingredients and blend until smooth.

Chocolaty Bean Smoothie

This isn't your everyday smoothie, that's for sure! Black beans give this recipe a solid foundation. With almost 8 grams of protein from the black beans alone, this high-powered smoothie may be the one you want to drink after some serious strength training.

1 TABLESPOON UNSWEETENED NATURAL COCOA POWDER

1 FROZEN BANANA

½ CUP COOKED BLACK BEANS, DRAINED AND RINSED

⅓ CUP LOW-FAT CHOCOLATE MILK (REGULAR OR ALMOND)

2 MEDJOOL DATES

3 ICE CUBES

In a blender, combine all ingredients and blend until smooth.

Note: This recipe has higher caloric content and the serving size is smaller.

Goji Berry Dream 1

Goji berries are truly a dream when it comes to any weight-loss program. These berries are the only fruit that contain all essential amino acids—and they contain more protein than any other fruit (4 grams per ounce)! Sometimes called a superfood, goji berries are a better source of iron than spinach and are anti-inflammatory, antibacterial, and antifungal.

¼ CUP GOJI BERRIES

½ CUP WATER

1 CUP CHOPPED CANTALOUPE

1½ CUPS BABY KALE

1 SMALL CARROT, PEELED AND CHOPPED

½ SMALL FROZEN BANANA

Soak the goji berries in the water for approximately 10 minutes. In a blender, combine berries with remaining ingredients and blend until smooth. Add more water if desired.

Goji Berry Dream 2

The goji berries and chia seeds are great protein sources in this tangerine smoothie. The tangerines produce a drink that's bursting with sweetness and tang—a nice alternative to oranges.

⅓ CUP GOJI BERRIES

1 CUP COCONUT WATER

2 TANGERINES, PEELED AND SEEDED

5 CUPS FRESH BABY SPINACH

1 LARGE CARROT, PEELED AND CHOPPED

1 TABLESPOON CHIA SEEDS

Soak the goji berries in the coconut water for 10 minutes. In a blender, combine berries with remaining ingredients until smooth.

Hot Lime and Mango Smoothie

This hearty smoothie is full of substance and is designed to give you protein with a little kick! Jalapeño peppers can kick-start your metabolism for a burn not only in your mouth but also in your body. Flax and hemp have anti-inflammatory properties, which are essential when you're working out.

JUICE OF ½ LIME

½ BANANA

½ CUP FROZEN MANGO

¼ JALAPEÑO, SEEDED AND CHOPPED

1 CUP LOW-FAT REGULAR OR ALMOND MILK

1 TABLESPOON GOLDEN FLAXSEED MEAL

1 TABLESPOON HEMP SEED

In a blender, combine all ingredients and blend until smooth.

Powered by Tofu

No need to be scared of tofu! A healthy source of protein from the soybean plant, tofu provides 10 grams of protein per ½ cup. In rural China, soybeans are a major source of protein in the diet. Tofu makes this smoothie extra creamy and extra delicious!

1 CUP MIXED FROZEN BERRIES

½ CUP LOW-FAT SILKEN TOFU

⅛ CUP POMEGRANATE JUICE

4 MEDJOOL DATES

½ TEASPOON FINELY GRATED, PEELED FRESH GINGER ROOT

In a blender, combine all ingredients and blend until smooth.

Quinoa-Banana Smoothie

This smoothie delivers more than 8 grams of protein. Quinoa is one of two complete plant-based proteins (soy is the other), and it is rich in micronutrients too.

½ CUP COOKED QUINOA

1 CUP LOW-FAT REGULAR OR SOY MILK

1 FROZEN BANANA

2 MEDJOOL DATES

¾ TEASPOON PURE VANILLA EXTRACT

½ TEASPOON GROUND CINNAMON

DASH OF ALLSPICE

In a blender, combine quinoa and milk and blend for 30 seconds. Add fruit and spices and blend until smooth. Add ground cinnamon for garnish if desired.

Red Bush Tea Smoothie

*Rooibos (red bush) tea is an herb tea loaded with antioxidants and minerals.
Combined with the antioxidant power of blueberries and the essential fatty
acids and protein of flax and hemp, this smoothie is just what the nutritionist
ordered to meet your protein needs.*

2 CUPS RED BUSH TEA, CHILLED

½ BANANA

½ CUP FROZEN BLUEBERRIES

1 TABLESPOON GOLDEN FLAXSEED MEAL

1 TABLESPOON HEMP SEEDS

Pour tea into a blender, add the fruit and seeds, and blend until smooth.

CHAPTER 12

Digestive Health Smoothies

Apple-Mango Spice Smoothie

A soothing combination of apples, mangos, veggies, and spices makes for a digestive smoothie that not only soothes and heals, but also tastes great.

½ APPLE, PEELED, CORED, AND CHOPPED, THEN FROZEN

½ CUP WATER

½ CUP APPLE JUICE

¼ TEASPOON GROUND CINNAMON

⅛ TEASPOON VANILLA EXTRACT

⅛ TEASPOON GROUND NUTMEG

¼ CUCUMBER, PEELED

1 CUP FRESH SPINACH

½ CUP FROZEN MANGO

½ CUP ICE

In a blender, combine apple, water, and apple juice and blend for 30 seconds. Add the remaining ingredients and blend until smooth.

Berry-Lemon Slushie

Especially good on a hot summer day, this lemon juice slushie/smoothie nourishes and refreshes. Lemon juice has been credited with fighting tumors, facilitating faster healing, and aiding in the digestive process. Some people like more lemon juice than others, so experiment a little with the amount you use. (And if you have a little extra, lemon juice is an effective cleaning product, too!)

¼ CUP LEMON JUICE

⅛ CUP COLD WATER

1 CUP FROZEN STRAWBERRIES

1 CUP RASPBERRIES

¾ CUP ICE

In a blender, combine all ingredients and blend until smooth.

Blackberry Cream Smoothie

Blackberries may be the berry of choice when it comes to healthy digestion. The tannins they contain help decrease inflammation in the GI tract, rid the body of hemorrhoids, and ease diarrhea. And cardamom—which adds a little kick to this smoothie—can help fight nausea as well as a host of other digestive ailments.

½ CUP FROZEN BLACKBERRIES

½ CUP LOW-FAT YOGURT (REGULAR OR SOY)

½ CUP LOW-FAT REGULAR OR SOY MILK

4 MEDJOOL DATES

¼ TEASPOON GROUND CARDAMOM

WATER, AS NEEDED

In a blender, combine all ingredients and blend until smooth. Add water if desired.

Grapefruit, Apple, and Ginger Smoothie

This smoothie aids in digestion by ridding the body of gas and relaxing the GI tract. Ginger can take credit for that; it also acts as an antioxidant and an anti-inflammatory. An added bonus: An ounce of ginger has only 4 calories!

½ SWEET APPLE, PEELED, CORED, AND CHOPPED

½-INCH PIECE FRESHLY PEELED GINGER ROOT

½ CUP WATER

½ GRAPEFRUIT

1 CUP FROZEN STRAWBERRIES

In a blender, combine apple, ginger, and water. Pulse quickly, then add the remaining ingredients and blend until smooth.

In-the-Tropics Smoothie

You may not actually be in the tropics, but you'll certainly feel like it when sipping on this drink. The ease with which this smoothie goes down only adds to its relaxing effect. Pineapple is full of bromelain, a digestive aid often added to digestive enzymes.

2 LARGE KALE LEAVES, STEMMED AND CHOPPED

¼ CUP CHOPPED PINEAPPLE

¼ CUP PINEAPPLE JUICE

½ CUP LOW-FAT REGULAR OR ALMOND MILK

½ FROZEN BANANA

In a blender, combine all ingredients and blend until smooth.

Papaya-Berry Smoothie

This smoothie can be made with either fresh or frozen fruit, or a combination of both. Regardless of whether you use fresh or frozen papaya, this smoothie will go down easily and digest well. Why? Because papaya contains papain, an enzyme frequently added to proteolytic enzymes (enzymes used to digest proteins).

½ CUP BLACKBERRIES

½ CUP BLUEBERRIES

½ CUP CHOPPED FRESH OR FROZEN PAPAYA

⅛ TEASPOON GROUND CINNAMON

WATER, AS NEEDED

In a blender, combine all ingredients and blend until smooth. Add water if desired.

Mango-Cherry Smoothie

In addition to being full of antioxidants, mangos are a great source of malic acid, tartaric acid, and citric acid. These acids have all been found to help the body maintain an alkaline state and contribute to a balanced intestinal flora and a healthy digestive tract.

1 CUP FROZEN MANGO

1½ CUPS FROZEN DARK SWEET CHERRIES

1 SMALL FROZEN BANANA

½ CUP FROZEN PEACHES

2 MEDJOOL DATES

WATER, AS NEEDED

In a blender, combine all ingredients and blend until smooth. Add a small amount of water if desired.

Persimmon-Berry Smoothie

The persimmon, though it seems like a fruit, is technically a berry. Perhaps this berry's claim to fame is its role in fighting eye degeneration, namely retinal damage, cataracts, and age-related macular degeneration (ARMD). In terms of digestive health, persimmons can help prevent sluggish bowels and constipation. It is sold in two varieties: Hachiya or Fuyu. Hachiyas must be eaten when they're very soft and ripe, whereas Fuyus are best when a little firm.

3 PERSIMMONS, PEELED AND SEEDED

1 CUP ORANGE JUICE

½ CUP FROZEN BERRIES

In a blender, combine all ingredients and blend until smooth.

Pumpkin Fall Smoothie

Pumpkin (or pumpkin purée) is a great choice for digestive health. Pumpkin provides a good amount of dietary fiber, an essential component of healthy digestion. And the potassium in pumpkin contributes to your digestive needs too.

¾ CUP LOW-FAT VANILLA YOGURT (REGULAR OR SOY)

½ CUP CRUSHED ICE

¼ CUP PUMPKIN PURÉE

¼ RIPE BANANA

4 MEDJOOL DATES

¼ TEASPOON PUMPKIN PIE SPICE

⅛ TEASPOON VANILLA EXTRACT

WATER (OPTIONAL)

In a blender, combine the yogurt and ice and blend for 30 seconds. Add the purée and blend for an additional 30 seconds. Add the remaining ingredients and water, if needed, and blend until smooth.

Know Your Produce

WHAT TO BUY ORGANIC

Organic foods are almost always preferable to their conventionally grown counterparts, since no chemical fertilizers or pesticides are used to grow them. There are many conventionally produced foods that contain only low levels of these toxins, but there are several that consistently contain high levels.

If possible, you should always shop for the organic versions of the following twenty foods.

Apples

Conventional growers use more than forty different pesticides on their apples, as insects and fungus threaten crops. Pesticide residue is found not just on fresh apples, but in apple products such as applesauce and apple juice.

Bell Peppers

Bell peppers are treated with almost fifty different pesticides intended to keep insects and fungus away. These thin-skinned vegetables are difficult to clean completely, so be sure to use only organic ones.

Blueberries

Blueberries might be powerfully nutritious, but conventionally grown varieties can't be trusted. Choose organic blueberries, even if that means you have to buy frozen ones. As a bonus, frozen varieties are easier to store and add cool goodness to smoothies.

Celery

Celery is heavily treated with pesticide, and that pesticide drips down into the plant's ribs. Tests conducted by the U.S. Department of Agriculture (USDA) has found more than sixty different pesticides tainting celery.

Cherry Tomatoes

Bugs love to eat cherry tomatoes, and the fruit is also woefully susceptible to fungal attack. Cherry tomatoes are treated with a toxic cocktail of pesticides, making them one of the dirtiest plant foods on the market. Try growing your own during the summer.

Coffee

Coffee, including green coffee extract, sometimes makes its way into green smoothies, and many of us enjoy our morning cup of joe. To stay on the safe side, choose fair trade-certified and Rainforest Alliance–labeled organic coffee; it is grown without pesticides.

Collard Greens

Just like kale and spinach, collard greens are often treated with a mind-boggling array of pesticides. The USDA has revealed that there are as many as forty-five different chemicals commonly used on collards. Organic collard greens can be found in many places. If you can't find them, try cabbage or Brussels sprouts instead.

Cucumbers

Cucumbers are among the dirtiest types of produce on the market, unless they're organic. More than thirty-five different pesticides are used to treat these green beauties. If you can't find organic ones, peeling the skin off will greatly reduce your chances of exposure, but it will also eliminate many of the plant's nutrients.

Grapes

Grapes are a favorite with people everywhere, but since they are susceptible to fungus and insect attack, farmers often raise them conventionally, using as many as thirty different pesticides in the process. Grapes should always be purchased organic; there's just no way to eliminate all the residue.

Hot Peppers

Hot peppers such as jalapeños are often coated in a toxic sheen of pesticide. Buy them organic, or don't buy them at all.

Kale

Yet another of the best leafy green vegetables for smoothies, kale is quite hardy, but conventional farmers treat it with pesticides anyway. Luckily, this popular plant is very easy to find in farmers' markets and at grocery stores, proudly bearing an organic label.

Lettuce

Like other leafy green vegetables, lettuce is a favorite with bugs of all kinds, so conventional farmers resort to spraying it with a toxic blend of more than fifty different pesticides. Organic lettuce is very easy to find at grocery stores and in farmers' markets, and it's very easy to grow in a container or in a small garden.

Meat

No one puts meat in smoothies, but what you eat when you aren't drinking smoothies is just as important as what makes its way into your glass. Since beef and other meat animals are given a steady diet of pesticide-laden food, the pesticides bioaccumulate inside their body fat, eventually making their way into your food. If you eat pork, beef, chicken, turkey, or other meat, select only organic options.

Milk

Like meat, milk contains high levels of pesticides. In fact, tests have shown as many as twelve different ones contaminating conventionally produced milk. Choose organic milk or select a nut or soy milk instead.

Nectarines

Nectarines, particularly those imported from other countries, are laced with as many as thirty-three different pesticides. Choose organic ones or select a different fruit to use in your smoothies.

Peaches

Like nectarines, peaches are covered in a toxic film of pesticides. Testing has shown more than sixty types of pesticides on peaches. Thanks to their fuzzy skin, peaches are particularly difficult to clean. Buy them organic, or select a different type of fruit.

Potatoes

Luckily, most people don't include potatoes in smoothies, but because these mineral-rich vegetables are a favorite at dinnertime, they make the list. Testing has shown there are more than thirty-five different pesticides used on potatoes, with russets being among the filthiest. Sweet potatoes are a good substitute.

Spinach

Unfortunately, one of the most reliable green smoothie ingredients has a constant presence on the toxic list. Often treated with as many as fifty different pesticides, this leafy green is impossible to clean and should be eaten only if it is organic. Fortunately, organic spinach, including many prewashed and prepackaged options, is readily available at an affordable price.

Strawberries

Strawberries grow close to the ground and are susceptible to attack by both insects and fungal diseases. Farmers use almost sixty different pesticides to keep their berries from being ruined, and it's nearly impossible to get them completely clean. Choose organic strawberries, even if that means you have to buy them frozen rather than fresh.

Zucchini

This popular summer squash has a thin skin and is a favorite with pests, so conventional farmers use an array of pesticides to keep bugs away. Organic zucchini is easy to find and is a plant anyone can grow with minimal effort.

A GUIDE TO SEASONAL SHOPPING

As the seasons change, so does the produce available at local farmers' markets. There are many fruits and vegetables that are best and freshest at certain times of the year. Produce availability will vary based on where you live.

Spring

Artichokes

Arugula

Asparagus

Beets

Blueberries

Carrots

Cauliflower

Cherries

Cilantro

Collard greens

Fennel

Fiddlehead ferns

Garlic

Green onions

Kale

Kohlrabi

Leeks

Lettuce

Mint

Mushrooms

Onions

Parsley

Pea sprouts

Peas

Potatoes

Rhubarb

Snow peas

Strawberries

Swiss chard

Turnip greens

Turnips

Summer

Apricots

Avocados

Basil

Beet greens

Beets

Bell peppers

Blackberries

Blueberries

Broccoli

Cantaloupe

Carrots

Cauliflower

Cherries

Cilantro

Collard greens

Corn

Fennel

Figs

Gooseberries

Green beans

Honeydew melon

Hot peppers

Kale

Lettuce

Nectarines

Peaches

Pears

Peas

Plums

Rhubarb

Snow peas

Summer squash

Swiss chard

Tomatoes

Watermelon

Zucchini

Autumn

Apples

Artichokes

Arugula

Beet greens

Beets

Belgian endive

Blackberries

Blueberries

Broccoli

Brussels sprouts

Butternut squash

Cauliflower

Celery

Celery root

Collard greens

Eggplant

Fennel

Figs

Garlic

Grapes

Kale

Kohlrabi

Lettuce

Parsnips

Pears

Persimmons

Potatoes

Pumpkins

Radicchio

Radishes

Rhubarb

Rutabagas

Spaghetti squash

Spinach

Sweet potatoes

Swiss chard

Tomatoes

Zucchini

Winter

Beet greens

Beets

Belgian endive

Broccoli

Brussels sprouts

Butternut squash

Cabbage

Carrots

Cauliflower

Celery

Celery root

Collard greens

Curly endive

Fennel

Garlic
Kale
Leeks
Onions
Parsnips
Persimmons
Potatoes

Pumpkins
Radicchio
Rutabagas
Spaghetti squash
Sweet potatoes
Turnip greens
Turnips

Index

pineapple juice, 66
pineapple
    in antioxidant smoothies, 44
    in breakfast smoothies, 22–23
    in cleansing smoothies, 28, 30–32
    in digestive health smoothies, 66
    in green smoothies, 35, 37
    in high-energy smoothies, 52–53
    in low-fat smoothies, 44, 47
plums, 37
pomegranate juice, 43, 56, 61
preparation tips, 17–18
produce shopping tips, 69–75
    organic produce, 69–72
    seasonal produce, 73–75
protein smoothies, 57–62
    Banana-Oat Smoothie, 58
    Berry Fruity Tofutti, 58
    Chocolaty Bean Smoothie, 59
    Goji Berry Dream 1, 59
    Goji Berry Dream 2, 60
    Hot Lime and Mango Smoothie, 60
    Powered by Tofu, 61
    Quinoa-Banana Smoothie, 61
    Red Bush Tea Smoothie, 62
    weight loss facilitation with, 10
pumpkin purée, 68

Q

quinoa, 61

R

raspberries, 28–29, 41–42, 49, 54, 64
red bush tea, 62
refined carbohydrates, 10
rest, adequate vs. inadequate, 13
rolled oats, 41, 58
rooibos tea, 62

S

seasonal produce shopping tips, 73–75
Smoothie Diet
    antioxidant smoothies, 39–44
    beneficial ingredients, 5
    breakfast smoothies, 21–26
    cleansing smoothies, 27–32
    detrimental ingredients, 5–6
    digestive health smoothies, 63–68
    green smoothies, 33–38
    health benefits of, 3–4
    high-energy smoothies, 51–56
    low-fat smoothies, 45–50
    produce shopping tips, 69–75
    protein smoothies, 57–62
    ten-day meal plan, 17–20
    three-day detox, 15–16
    tips for. *See* tips
    weight loss with, 9–13
soy milk
    in antioxidant smoothies, 44
    in breakfast smoothies, 23–24, 26
    in digestive health smoothies, 65
    in high-energy smoothies, 53, 55
    in protein smoothies, 58, 61
spinach, 34–35, 37, 43, 56, 64. *See also* baby spinach
strawberries, 39–44
    in antioxidant smoothies, 49–44
    in breakfast smoothies, 23, 25
    in cleansing smoothies, 28–29
    in digestive health smoothies, 64–65
    in green smoothies, 34, 36
    in low-fat smoothies, 46
sweet potatoes, 55

T

tangerine juice, 36
tangerines, 35, 60
ten-day meal plan, 17–20
    day-by-day menus, 19–20
    dinner suggestions for, 18–19
    preparation tips for, 17–18
thermic effect of food (TEF), 10
three-day detox, 15–16
tips
    goal-setting, 12
    motivational, 12–13
    preparation, 17–18
    produce shopping, 69–75.
        See also produce shopping tips
    smoothie-making skills, 6–7
    weight loss, 9–13
tofu, 58, 61
tomatoes, 38, 43, 46
toxic twenty foods, 69–72
toxins, 15–16

W

watermelon, 36, 52–54
weight-loss tips, 9–13
    motivational, 12–13
    nutrient-dense smoothies, 9–12
white grape juice, 58

Y

yogurt
    in antioxidant smoothies, 44
    in breakfast smoothies, 25
    in cleansing smoothies, 28
    in digestive health smoothies, 65, 68
    in high-energy smoothies, 52
    in low-fat smoothies, 48–49
    in protein smoothies, 58

Printed in Great Britain
by Amazon

82453908R00051